MW01633504
Prepare!
Embracing seasons of singleness by actively preparing yourself for your future spouse.
Kenzie Mormile

Prepare!

Embracing the time of singleness by actively

preparing yourself to love another person as Christ loves.

Cover & Graphic Design: Kenzie Mormile

Koluna Creative LLC.

ISBN-10: 0-9977408-0-9

ISBN-13: 978-0-9977408-0-6

theovernightmom.com

Available on Amazon.com and other retail outlets.

My Family:

I am very grateful to all of you for being by my side through it all! I love you and I am blessed to have you all in my life!

Katie, Gladson & Pubs:

I appreciate your friendship, advice, being there for me and brightening up some of my most difficult days, and listening to me complain about my singleness. :-) Thank you for everything!

Father Jay, Theresa & Life Teen Core:

Thank you for bringing light to the trueness, goodness and beauty of the Catholic Church and for educating me about why we believe what we believe.

To my Husband, Mario:

Thank you for loving me, believing in me, and for always seeking to become the best version of yourself.

I love you.

Table of Contents

Starting the Conversation

I am going to cut to the chase: are you single, lonely, and unhappy? No? Excellent! Praise God for that! Yes? Know that my heart aches for you in your suffering and you are especially dear to me.

Marriage, dating, and relationships have been on the forefront of my mind ever since my earliest memories. I spent hours daydreaming about getting married and starting a family of my own some day. When I was a mere 3 years of age, I had my first crush on a little boy in the neighborhood. I remember thinking to myself,

"He's cute and nice. I want him to be my boyfriend!" At such a young age, I probably should have been concerned about cooties or playing with my toys, but I remember, even then, having a difficult time shaking the desire to have a significant other.

Eventually the boy's family moved and we lost contact, not that it mattered because I was way too shy to make a move. I recall thinking, "That's okay, I will find somebody else when I am a few years older!" As the years passed by, I continued to be enamored by people in relationships. I use to go out for ice cream with my dad and just sit, talk, and people watch. I would always become excited watching couples interact and having fun together. While still in pre-school, I remember being at my dance practices and recitals watching the older girls interact with their boyfriends. I would think, "I cannot wait until I am a little older and I can have one of my own." One night during a dance recital practice, my gorgeous dance teacher's boyfriend surprised her with a giant bouquet of flowers. It was one of those cute moments where everyone in the room simultaneously exclaimed, "Awwwww!" I wished so badly that one day I could have a relationship like that one. I saw the way they looked at each other. The effort he put into making her happy. I studied the way they reacted toward each other in different environments and the relationship always appeared genuine, healthy, fun, and loving. You could see in their faces, they were filled with joy. They spent time together practicing their dancing. He brought snacks for her after practices. He treated her exceptionally well, and was kind to everyone around him. It was through that couple that I began to fall in love with love.

Growing up, I was encouraged to follow the teachings of the Catholic Church. My parents divorced when I was only three years old, so I had many questions on my mind about love and marriage at a very early age. Despite my parent's divorce, I was taught that marriage is a forever promise between a man and a woman. I was told it is important to respect your future spouse by saving things for them. At the time, I wasn't quite sure what these specific "things" were, but I definitely was aware that kissing wasn't something to take lightly. During times I witnessed couples demonstrating unhealthy relationships, my family members made an effort to explain to me that what they were doing was wrong. I was incredibly lucky to have been taught the importance of making God the number one priority of my life and that the most successful relationships happen when He is a part of it. So I prayed. I remember being in kindergarten sitting in the church pews, slightly tired and bored while daydreaming of getting married some day. At that moment, I decided to pray that God would send me someone amazing and that I would meet him as soon as possible.

Over the years life happened and crushes developed, but I was always too afraid to admit that I had any interest in anyone. I knew that I was young and typically people with boyfriends were in High School, so I prepared to wait until then to become concerned with finding someone and had faith that God would bring the right person to me whenever the timing worked and I was ready. Oh, to have the trust of a child. I had all of the confidence in the world that I would be in a fantastic relationship some day until I was in early middle school when I over heard some classmates talking about how a few of our friends were "boyfriend and girlfriend." I couldn't believe it. This was happening already? I didn't think people entered into relationships until high school! I felt completely unprepared and rushed. If my friends were starting to have boyfriends - I needed one too!

During the next few years, *that* was my mentality. At sleepovers we would discuss the boys we liked and there would always be a few girls who insisted they didn't have crushes, or that we were too young to "date." I could never understand that outlook as I always wanted to find someone to share my life with: someone to love and to be loved by.

As the middle school years passed, I began to find myself becoming more and more emotionally hurt. I was painfully shy when it came to telling boys I was interested and it seemed as if all the ones I was attracted to had interest in other girls. During the few circumstances when feelings were most likely mutual, both of us were too afraid to be open about our feelings - so nothing ever came about.

When high school arrived, I thought for sure I would find someone awesome and the experience would be exactly how it is in movies. Boy, was I wrong. I spent a majority of those years watching other girls find guys who had mutual interest. I was sad, lonely, and increasingly feeling hurt. I was upset that no one seemed to desire a relationship with me. I began to question whether something was wrong with me. Was I too ugly? Too short? Too reserved? Too pale? Too this and too that. Over time, I projected the numerous qualities I speculated about what prospective love interests may have thought of me and began to identify myself in that way. I never felt confident in my own skin. I went through my days never feeling comfortable enough to be my authentic self.

Other issues began to arise. In certain respects, I began to socially isolate myself. I didn't understand why I was growing so depressed, why I was feeling deeply hurt, and why life was not playing out as I had imagined. Through this, I began to become upset with God. Hoping for a potential husband was a good and moral thing. Praying and asking for this desire I longed for with all my heart, was good and righteous as well. I prayed for years asking in full confidence for this desire. But I received nothing. Not only was I single, but I was miserable - and it hurt.

I needed hope. I began to find that "hope" in fantasizing about having a relationship. I truly believed that having a boyfriend would solve all of my problems and eliminate the pain I had been feeling for so long. After all, everyone I witnessed in relationships appeared incredibly happy. I didn't need friends or family, or even God. All I needed to do in order to be happy is to find a boyfriend - or so I thought.

Since my prayers had not yet been answered, I began struggling in my spiritual life. All of my prayers were directed at finding a companion. During my prayer time, I was constantly bargaining with God in an attempt to make Him grant my desires (when and how I wanted them). God is not a genie, yet I was treating

Him that way and wondering why He wasn't coming through for me. I read the Bible daily in an effort to grow in my faith. The more I grew closer to Christ, the less appealing potential boyfriends around me grew to be. I was desperately seeking love but at the same time I wasn't desperate enough to settle. I started noticing how most guys my age did not have pure thoughts or use wholesome language. They were caught up in getting physically involved with girls, partying, and in temporary pleasures. The more I realized how distant the people at school were from Christ, the more I started to realize a boy was not the cure to my misfortune. Only God was.

But I was alone. Extremely alone. Deeply hurt, profoundly confused and not to mention, an emotional wreck. Through a series of events, I was invited to a Catholic Life Teen youth retreat. I loved God and was interested in growing stronger in my faith. However, I did not want to go. As I contemplated the invitation, I thought to myself, "If I don't go, I am just going to be alone at home sitting in my room eating a giant bowl of ice cream." So I went, and through a deep surprise encounter by my Creator during Eucharistic Adoration my heart was touched in a very powerful way and my life changed forever.

From that point forward, I reevaluated my goals in life. Loving, knowing, glorifying, and having a relationship with God became the absolute priority. I didn't care whether or not I "found love." Loving God and knowing He loved me was enough. His grace was completely enough for me. I felt whole and made new again. I still had a lot of work to do in becoming the best version of myself I could possibly be - but I was changed and this transformation affected all of my relationships.

The more I relinquished control, the more wonderful people and opportunities were brought into my life. Though I never managed to "officially" be in a serious relationship, I grew close to guys and learned a ton about life and relationships. I had friendships with men who hurt me, helped me, manipulated me, comforted me, tried to corrupt me, encouraged me, tore me down, built me up, criticized me, complimented me, led me on and came on too strong. Through time and experience, I managed to become excellent at staying away from people I knew would not be a good match for me. I formed relationships with men who were truly genuine, kind, and good people overall.

My desire for marriage continued to remain strong as life continued on. It became a huge spiritual struggle.

I was following Church teachings as best as I possibly could and focusing on building up my relationship with Christ, yet I was still struggling to find a mutual match. I would meet solid, amazing Christian men that were wonderful and I liked very much, yet something didn't make me feel fully at peace. I strived for a good and holy romantic love, yet couldn't find it anywhere. Was I doing something wrong? What do I do? Where are the answers?

It was a challenging place to be. I knew I was called to married life, yet I didn't know how to discern and prepare to follow that call. I didn't know how to go about the dating process or how to find a spouse. I felt uneasy sitting back and not actively taking action in an effort to pursue a potential person. I questioned whether or not my standards were too high and whether or not finding someone who is an ideal match for me would be unattainable.

Through a roller coaster of emotions, events, and experiences, God led me to my husband. It is unbelievable how perfect he is for me. He compliments my life and way of doing things. He has my same core beliefs and values, shared goals, and is truly the man God had planned for me. There are many tiny things about him and who he is that demonstrate how God not only answers our prayers, but He answers them in intricate, detailed ways. Little qualities I wanted in a spouse in terms of physical appearance, distance from where I preferred to live, career path, desire for children, along with many other things were all answered in him.

As I live out the sacrament of Holy Matrimony, I am in awe of how God has worked in my life. I reflect back upon the girl crying in her college dorm room; sad, hurt, lonely, confused, looking for concrete advice and answers. From a Catholic perspective, we are provided with tons of content and guidance about how to be in a relationship; the importance of staying pure, mutual respect, and having a common belief system. However, we do not have many resources on what to do specifically when a person finds him or herself called to married life but without a partner.

This is important. So many people are finding themselves settling for those who do not help them reach their fullest potential. Both women and men remain in unhealthy relationships out of loneliness, or fear of never finding someone else. This is why we find such large numbers of young people turning to drugs and alcohol. Mother Teresa says it best, "The greatest disease in the West today is not tuberculosis or leprosy; it is being unwanted, unloved, and uncared for. We can cure physical diseases with medicine, but the only cure for loneliness, despair, and hopelessness is love. There are many in the world who are dying for a piece of bread but there are many more dying for a little love. The poverty in the West is a different kind of poverty. It is not only a poverty of loneliness but also of spirituality. There's a hunger for love, as there is a hunger for God."

We need to start the conversation. We need to encourage one another to pursue greatness. We don't need to spend our time of singleness being sad and feeling sorry for ourselves. We don't need to sit around waiting for a potential spouse to fall out of the sky right in front of our faces. We need to be proactive. We need to prepare. We are actively called to love.

Happiness Starts Now

If there is anything I've learned from my years of singleness and from observing others, it is that our feeling of satisfaction and overall contentment cannot and will not derive from an external source. It can be easy to justify our discontentment by thinking, "When ____ happens, my life will get better." Or, "As soon as ____ happens, I will finally be happy!" A great majority of the time the, "if-my-circumstances-were-different-I-would-be-happier" mentality ends with disappointment when true joy is not found.

Relationships, particularly romantic ones, are a beautiful thing. There is something fascinating about witnessing a couple interact; laughing together, encouraging each other and enjoying life together. Because of this, many singles fall into the trap of thinking once they find a person to love and be in a relationship with, they will find happiness. Unfortunately, this is false. Our happiness is not dependent on our circumstances, it is dependent upon our faith in Christ along with the joy of knowing, loving, and having a personal relationship with Him. Until you can learn to be truly joyful alone, you are not fully prepared mentally, emotionally, or spiritually ready to be in a serious relationship with another person. Happiness begins right now. Focus on living joyfully!

So if I feel fully happy and content in Christ, why do I still have the strong desire for a relationship? This was one of the biggest questions I had for years.

As I mentioned before, throughout my whole life, I wanted to get married and have children. During college, I would mention this desire to friends assuming they felt the same way. I was shocked to find out that many of them didn't think marriage was a big deal, and several had absolutely no desire to *ever* have children. Many people laughed when I said I wanted to have a family with many children. It deeply hurt my heart to see these girl friends of mine looking happy in their relationships knowing that almost every one of them was on birth control, sleeping with their boyfriends, and had no plans of a committed, life-long future together. How come I am trying my best to honor God and "do things right"*and* I have a stronger desire than all of them for marriage and having a family, yet I am eternally single (so it seemed at least) and they are continuously in relationships?! It felt extremely unfair. Beyond that, I started to question whether or not it was normal or right to have such an intense desire for marriage and family life.

Why do we have the desire to be in a romantic relationship? "The Lord God said, 'It is not good for the man to be alone; I will make him a helper suitable for him' (Genesis 2: 18)." The Lord proceeds to take one of the man's ribs to create the woman. Because of this, "A man leaves his father and mother and clings to his wife, and the two of them become one flesh (Genesis 2:24)." Men and women have been created to compliment each other and work together in harmony. What a beautiful design! We have literally been created for each other.

We are designed to be in communion with others, outside of our own selves. God declared and instituted the

Church to be the Body of Christ, "Now you are the body of Christ and individually members of it." (1 Corinthians 12:27). Sin separates. It isolates us, tears us away from God and prevents us from being all that we are fully capable of being. When we embrace our call to live beyond our individual desires we are able to live fuller, more loving, unifying lives of love.

Having a romantic partner can be a life-giving, mutually beneficial relationship, provided that Christ is at the center. Aside from those who have been given the gift of embracing the vocation of singleness or Holy Orders, our desire for a union with a romantic companion is a response to our call to bear life, raise God-loving, joyful children and teach them the faith. This desire is a good thing. Marriage calls each couple to be a visible sign of Christ's love in the world. It is a special vocation that should not be taken lightly.

Called to be Holy:

Should I Become a Nun?

The first time I contemplated becoming a nun was in the 8th grade as I was preparing for the sacrament of Confirmation. Although I was mostly "going through the motions" at the time, I read the Bible often, trying my best to do what was right and refrain from sinning. Prior to being confirmed, I was standing in a line with the other confirmation candidates when a nun came up to me. She struck up a conversation saying, "Out of everyone here, I can see you becoming a nun the most. Be open to it." Wow. There's something powerful about a nun telling you that you would make a great nun that plants the idea in your mind to start considering it. Though it was never my ideal vocation, I remained open to it. I put it to prayer only to find it was not the vocation God best prepared me to serve Him in. Once I realized being called to married life required not only my own surrendering to God's call, but the mutual openness of another person, I was in a bit of a predicament.

Throughout high school, college, and beyond, several people have commented to me about how I should become a nun. They would often say they could see me becoming a nun because they consider me to be so "Holy."

Hmm... so let me get this straight: because I am the "holiest" of all of our friends; avoid using inappropriate language, don't sleep around, never tried drugs, I'm someone who is honest, kind, and goes to church, I should become a nun?! At what point did we, as Catholics, decide that all priests and nuns need to be as holy and as "perfect" as possible, but there is an unwritten rule that married people have permission to be lukewarm in their faith? It is as if priests and nuns are set aside as the special "Holy Ones"and marriage is a "lesser" or "default" vocation. Please do not misunderstand me. Priests and nuns are fantastic, holy people who lay down their lives for Christ. But so are married people. In fact, I would argue that it is even more important to have holy, Catholic husbands and wives. After all, priests and nuns are born out of the family unit. With the divorce rate as high as it is, now, perhaps more than ever, married couples are needed to live out their lives as faithful, holy and true to the Gospel as they can.

As a result of our baptismal vows, all Christians are called to live lives of holiness. This divine calling is our vocation. Our vocation can be lived in marriage, consecrated single life, priesthood, or religious life. No one vocation is superior to or inferior to another. Each one is specifically placed on a person's heart according to their unique gifts and is strengthened sacramentally by God's grace. Each and every vocation is a commitment made to contribute to the life and mission of the Church, designed to glorify God and build His kingdom.

It is important to note the family is brought about by marriage. Parents, children, and extended family members form the church of the home, also known as the domestic church (or Ecclesia domestica in Latin if you want to be fancy). This is the primary place where the Church resides and flourishes; in the daily love, prayer, care, compassion, generosity, growth, sacrifice, forgiveness, and faith in the day-to-day lives of ordinary families. (CCC 1666)

When a man joins the seminary he is required to have a minimum of a bachelors degree (typically in religious studies, theology, or philosophy), pursue a graduate degree from a Catholic seminary, then go on to have pastoral assignments and practice masses to demonstrate his knowledge and abilities. It is a process that takes approximately 4-8 years fully dedicated to the vocation. For nuns, depending on the order, it takes an average 6 to 12 years of discernment and preparation. There are several concrete steps people are required to follow while pursuing religious vocations.

Considering marriage is a sacrament, and a vocation as well, why is there such little guidance leading up to the wedding ceremony? We have programs and requirements put in place during the time of engagement, but what about the years prior to meeting your spouse? How are we suppose to properly find the man or woman we are suppose to marry? The simple answer is by following God's Word: the teachings found in the Bible, thus growing in our spiritual life. This is much easier said than done, especially in the context of the dating scene. It can be easy to create our own rules and justify our immoral actions because it seems like there is no concrete way to go about navigating the time of singleness prior to entering a dating relationship. I propose a different mindset. It is important for people to actively prepare themselves for a successful relationship- even prior to meeting the person they decide to marry.

Living With Purpose

Two halves equal a whole, yes? If a husband and wife each contribute 50% to the unit, the relationship will work out great, right? WRONG! Two halves of the same item equate to a whole. However, men and women are united in that while they do merge to become one unit greater than themselves, they remain two individual whole units- not meant to "complete" each other but to compliment each other.

That's God's design. Beautiful, isn't it? Two individuals, equal in dignity that coincide with one another perfectly. In marriage, both spouses need to give 100% of themselves. After all, they totally love each other, do they not? Jesus demonstrated the greatest example of true love for us when He gave 100% of Himself: His entire life for us so that we could share in the joy of eternal life with Him in heaven. That's why it is love. Both parties should be giving 100% of themselves every day out of genuine love for one another.

Too often, singles who have the desire to be in a relationship are finding themselves feeling very broken. Their hearts may be aching, they may feel lonely or they may simply be in need of companionship. When I was single, I was more broken than I even realized at the time. I had the false notion that having a significant other would alleviate a great amount of my anxieties and issues. When I believed that I was lonely, I reasoned, "If I had a boyfriend, I would never feel this way." When I was looking for a date to an event or function I thought, "If only I had a boyfriend - then I wouldn't have to wrack my brain thinking of someone to invite to go with me."

I also used my lack of a significant other to justify bad behavior. When I didn't feel comfortable in my own skin I would think, "Well, if I had a boyfriend I would have the motivation to stay physically fit, and I would feel more attractive," and so on and so forth.

Years went by wondering why nothing ever fully clicked finding a good significant other until I had a thought that was revolutionary. I reflected upon how I was tired of being sad, moping around thinking about how much I wanted a boyfriend all of the time. Then it hit me: I am powerless! I cannot control anybody other than myself. Although my desire is to fall in love and get married, I cannot plan my life around someone feeling mutually about me or wanting to marry me. I cannot rely on men - I can only rely on God.

There was only one problem: I strongly wanted children. I felt the call to raise a family but it would be impossible to have a child without finding a husband. Then I devised a solution: adoption! Perfect! My plan was set. From that day forward, I would no longer worry about finding a man. I figured if it happened without me having to worry or try to make a relationship happen, great! But I knew I couldn't put my life on hold waiting for a man that may never come. I was living with the mentality that marriage was owed to me simply because I desired it. Enough of that.

My new plan: to save up some money for a few years and then adopt a child on my own. One of my college professors did something similar and she seemed like a joyful, wonderful mother. My mindset at this point was that I needed to become the best version of myself I could be in order to honor God, honor a potential future child, and for myself - not to impress any men.

I slowly began facing my fears. I knew if I never found anyone to marry and I did decide to adopt a child, I would be a single mother without the support of a husband. I would need to be really strong both mentally and physically. I would need to overcome many of my fears. In particular, the fear of being alone.

I used to be terrified of doing anything alone - and I mean *anything*. Eating, going to a social event, even going to Church alone terrified me. When I went off to college, many Sundays I would skip Mass. It was not because I didn't care or that I didn't want to go. The feeling of fear was so strong and overpowering that I couldn't bear to attend by myself. When I started to realize what a problem my lack of Mass attendance was starting to become in my life, I slowly forced myself to go alone.

During those days, the process of going to Church on my own would take place as follows: first, I would leave my dorm room at least an hour ahead of time. I would proceed to drive around the area of the Church while mentally preparing myself to go in. This was followed by a pep talk from my mom while I was on the phone with her in tears afraid of walking in alone. Slowly but surely, week by week, those phone calls became text messages of encouragement. Over time, I didn't need as much mental preparation to walk into the Church.

Today, not only do I go to Mass alone without thinking about it, but I often prefer to go alone. How amazing is that?! Since I conquered that fear, I can now meet up with other people at Mass; walking into the Church alone without any problems or second thoughts about it. Since I no longer miss Mass or hide in fear - I am closer to being the best version of myself - the best me I can possibly be. What is more attractive? A woman so consumed with insecurity and fear that she can't even go anywhere alone? Or, a confident, independent woman who doesn't need to rely upon other people to provide her with comfort or make her happy?

The moral of the story: you cannot fully give love to another person if you haven't learned to fully love and respect yourself yet. Embrace your time of singleness! Don't run from it or be a sour lemon. Use it to your best advantage to grow into the woman you were created to be. After hearing me complain about my singleness day after day, a good friend of mine once said, "Maybe you're single right now because God wants you all to Himself? Listen to Him."

Though I admit, I didn't like hearing that reasoning at the time, my friend made an excellent point. I needed to use that time alone to grow closer to Christ. I needed to build my relationship with Him instead of worrying about a relationship with another human being. I listened to his advice. I utilized my time of singleness to grow in my faith. I became involved with groups through the Church, read scripture daily, ramped up my prayer life, started reading books, and ate healthier. I did a multitude of things to improve my life and my self confidence.

Suddenly, I kid you not, I went from being lucky if there was one slightly creepy person potentially interested in me to 9 quality guys not just potentially interested, but actively pursuing me all at once. I'm not exaggerating- 9! It was a bit overwhelming but I believe it happened for a reason. When we love ourselves and glorify God through the way we live our lives and treat our bodies, we will attract people who do the same.

Forming Healthy Relationships

When Jesus was asked what the greatest of all the commandments was, he responded, "You shall love the Lord your God with all your heart, with all your soul, with all your mind, and with all your strength." He continued on to say, "You shall love your neighbor as yourself. There is no other commandment greater than these." (Mark 12:31)

It is often second nature to pour great deal of time and energy into fostering a healthy relationship with a significant other, but it is just as challenging to balance all of the many different relationships in our lives. It is important to remember, we are created to be people of community. Even once we meet our "perfect match" we are called to live lives of greatness and we cannot do that when we are closed-off inside of ourselves.

Committed relationships demand time and require our priorities to be adjusted. It is immensely important for single people to utilize the time of singleness to develop and nurture *all* relationships so when a potential future spouse does enter their life, they will already have experience tending to their loved ones and will not need to spend time patching up any damaged bonds. It is best to be full and whole. Prepared to love and to be loved.

Let's examine the different types of relationships we all have in our lives:

Christ

The most important relationship you will ever have is with Christ. He created you. He is there for you 24/7. He knew you before you were born (Jeremiah 1:5). He desires a relationship with you. He loves you unconditionally. When it comes to actively pursuing a relationship with the Lord it is often easier said than done. We know He loves us. We know He wants us. However, we often put Him on the back burner until our hearts are extra heavy - then we beg Him for His help. Sound familiar?

We have to remember that we are sinners. We are weak. We fail. We try our best, but we can't do it all. We're imperfect. God already knows this. We do not have to explain or justify our actions. It is our human condition. We are in dire need of a savior. That's what Christ offers to us when our hearts are open. He hears us, responds to us. We must listen to Him and respond as well. We must read His word and meditate on it in order to know Him better. We must pray daily and ask for the strength and wisdom we need (James 1:5).

When we have an intimate personal relationship with God, we are made more aware of His will. This makes it easier to follow His ways. Think about your relationship with your closest friends. When you are out and about, do you ever see something that reminds you of them, so you text them a picture of it? If they've given you advice, do you ever refer back to their conversations to help someone else out? It works the same with Christ. The more aware we are of His presence in our lives, the more we see Him and are reminded of His works in our daily lives. The more we read His word or follow His wisdom, the more we are able to help others.

Cultivate your relationship with Jesus Christ. The more you fall in love with Him the more you will be open to falling in love with others. He is our Go-To for advice, the Ultimate Confidant, Best Friend, Comforter, and Loving Father, "Don't be discouraged, Don't be dismayed, Fear not, I'll be with you wherever you go" (Isaiah 41:10).

Self

I vividly remember talking to my dad after reading a bed time story as a little girl. He said, "Kenzie, do you remember the order?"

"Yep!" I exclaimed, "God first, then mommy, daddy, my family, then friends, then everybody else, then me!"

"Great job, you've got it!" he replied.

I understand the message my dad was trying to teach me: put other people above yourself. It is an important message as it certainly is never good to be selfish. This mentality was very good for me in the sense of being aware of the needs of others and putting them before my own. However, over the years it morphed into a self-destructive mindset. I put myself at the bottom of the list. It was as if I needed to love myself the least- if at all. It wasn't until I was in my early 20's that I realized the importance of loving myself. For years, I was paranoid that loving my own self would be considered conceited or immoral. After all, pride is considered the deadliest sin. Why would I want to even come close to going down that path?

When Jesus talked about the greatest commandment of all, He quoted Deuteronomy 6:5 and said we are to love God with all our heart. But He also added the second greatest commandment: "You shall love your neighbor as yourself." (Mark 12:31). You cannot give away something you don't have. In the same way, how can someone love another person if they don't have any love for themselves?

It is healthy and necessary to genuinely and authentically love ourselves. When we learn to love ourselves in a positive way, we aren't catering to our selfishness or our own desires - that would not be love. To love and value ourself means we are appreciating our lives, our bodies, and viewing our own being as precious and beautiful. We are a creation of a Creator that made us not just good, but very good (Genesis 1:31).

In my life, learning to love myself meant intentionally taking time to grow in my faith. It meant taking care of my body by feeding myself nutritious foods. It meant commitment to physical activity and regularly working out. For example, I never ate fruit from when I was about 4 years old until age 22. I have always loved juice and apple sauce though. When I was about 19, I started forcing myself to eat bananas- but other than that I don't recall ever eating fruit. Fruit was never a part of my diet, period. No apples, no strawberries, nothing. I realized this was pathetic. I needed to make a change but fruit grossed me out so much! How could I possibly eat it? I noticed my issue with fruit was the texture. From there, I learned I actually enjoyed smoothies. It was then that I decided I could get my fruit intake in the form of a smoothie!

However, this required sacrifice. I had to prioritize smoothie making over milkshake making. I had to plan ahead and get all of the ingredients necessary and had to put effort into preparing a smoothie unlike eating chips or cookies. It was something I did not for my own enjoyment. I changed my diet because I love my body and I want to keep it healthy and functioning as best as it can.

Mentally, I had to learn to love myself by valuing my own thoughts and ideas. I had to love myself for who I truly am - a child of God. I couldn't worry about what other people had that I didn't have or what I wish I had. I had to view myself through the eyes of Christ. In doing that, I began to view other people through those eyes. Instead of holding back compliments to other people, I found myself scattering compliments around everywhere I went. Loving myself freed me from the bondage of comparison and jealousy. It helped me rely less on others and fully on God.

Friendships with Guys

If I had to specialize in one friendship area it would be having positive platonic friendships with members of the opposite sex. I didn't intend for it to be this way but over the years I have seemed to develop more close friendships with guys than I have with girls. One piece of advice a good friend and teacher suggested when discussing the challenges of single life was to befriend as many guys as I possibly could. Her reasoning was that being with men better enables you to understand the male mind a bit better and help identify what qualities you like and don't like in a potential spouse.

Over the years, I managed to form many friendships with guys. Though pretty much every one of those circumstances began with some sort of potential interest beyond a friendship, I was able to remain strictly friends without including any form of physical intimacy. For some people this is very difficult. For me, I knew how much I cared about my future spouse and anticipated having a husband (God willing) some day and I didn't want anything to distort or add baggage to my future marriage relationship.

In my friendships, I ensured that anything remotely physically intimate never happened to begin with. As much as some may try to deny it, holding hands leads to kissing. Kissing leads to touching. Touching leads to more intimate touching and then more. It can be a very slippery slope and easy to get caught up in. I didn't want to go down that path. Even though I had no idea who my future husband was, or even if I would have the privilege of having a husband some day, I knew even then that I loved him, whoever He would be. I fought my hardest to avoid intimacies with other people because I knew I would want someone who loved me enough to do the same for me.

Let me tell you - I am *so* glad I didn't become close with the guys I went on dates with physically, even in small, flirtatious ways. Being able to witness some of my good guy friends forming long term relationships with girlfriends and getting married knowing I didn't take anything away from them or "corrupt" them in the least is such a beautiful gift. I feel fully free and it's amazing.

Part of the reason I am writing this book is so that other people might have the encouragement to do what I did, sparing themselves from the pain and heartache that occurs from intimacy (even seemingly minor things) outside of marriage. It has also been freeing to have the ability to maintain healthy and positive friendships with guy friends without having to feel uncomfortable about them being considered my "ex" or the awkwardness of a relationship ending on bad terms.

By avoiding physical intimacy (as much as possible, even in little ways) with people of the opposite sex we are able to form a more genuine, intimate emotional connection. It provides opportunities to honor your future spouse, view each other as individuals with unique personalities - more than a hot body or sweet talker, prevents you from experiencing emotional damage. To top it off, you have an awesome friendship that can last a lifetime.

Friendships with Your Girl Friends

One of my favorite things about male/female friendships is the lack of drama. Ladies, you know what I am talking about. It always seems like girls are so competitive. Guy friends are a lot less work in that sense. After having several friendships that were not mutually beneficial, I use to think there wasn't much of a need for girl friends. Over time, I found myself caring less and less about my girl friends. Here and there, a friend would invite me to hang out. It wasn't until my mom pointed out that my mood improves after hanging out with my girl friends that I began to understand the need for friendships with people my own gender.

Friends help provide us with an outside perspective of our lives. This enables us to know ourselves better. They help influence us as individuals and keep us from being lonely. Studies have shown there is a direct link to friendships and our overall happiness. "Like iron sharpens iron so man sharpens man" (Proverbs 27:17).

One of the best friends I ever had was my college

roommate, Katie. Throughout college, she was always there to listen and help me when I felt discouraged or overwhelmed. When school was stressful and busy, she would find a way to make an adventure out of the little free time we had. One evening, went on a late night trip to the pet store to buy some fish. We often decorated our dorm for different holidays or just when we needed a fun pick-me-up. We always had an enjoyable time together despite the busyness and stress of school. It was nice that she had a lot of the same interests and personality traits as I had but the biggest blessing of all was having such a close friend of faith. Katie was someone I could go to Church with and share my beliefs with, without fear of judgement or starting a debate. While it is good to have friends of many faiths, I am a believer that your close circle of friends should have values and goals similar to yours or personality traits that you wish to achieve. We become who we are around and our friends have a dramatic influence on who we are to become. Don't be afraid to distance yourself from friends who have a negative influence on you. Rekindle friendships with people you've drifted away from due to distance, or time. Foster friendships with people who make you want to become a better and a more loving person.

Relationships with Family

We can choose our friends but we cannot choose our family. This creates difficulty for a lot of people. We need to work our hardest to patch up bad relationships in our family. Give everyone the benefit of the doubt, reach out to them and love them. A common problem I see in families is the lack of forgiveness. Lack of forgiveness, in my observation, is the largest cause of family brokenness. Nobody likes their trust breached. Nobody likes knowing someone they love has hurt them. This is especially prevalent in financial matters. Regardless of how our family members have wronged us, we need to use the pain as an opportunity to practice forgiveness. If you spend years holding grudges over family members how do you expect a marriage to last? I would be highly skeptical of starting a relationship with someone who has hatred toward anyone - especially a family member. Even if they did something horrible, it doesn't necessarily mean you have to be their best friend. At least be on terms where you can carry a short conversation to acknowledge their value as a person, as a child of God.

Loving Everyone– Even Strangers

Of course, we must love all of the people around us!

Yes, even strangers. We need to be involved with our church community and the community around us. Being sympathetic to the needs of others is immensely important too. One person who did this exceptionally well was Mother Teresa. She once said, "I have found the paradox, that if you love until it hurts, there can be no more hurt, only more love." We need to love everyone around us. The more we do that the more we are able to give love to our families, our friends, and our significant others. "There will always be poor people in the land. Therefore I command you to be openhanded toward your fellow brothers who are poor and needy in your land." (Deuteronomy 15:11)

There is always love to give to the people around us. Have you ever heard someone say a good way to tell if your date is a good person is to pay attention on how they treat the waiter at dinner? That is so true! If a person isn't treating the strangers with respect and dignity, why do you expect them to do the same for you?

One of the things I first noticed about Mario, my husband, was on our first date when our waitress seemed a little bit grumpy. He commented on her behavior and then said, "Let's make it our goal to get her smiling by the end of this dinner." Sure enough, he got her smiling. She ended up sharing with us that she recently had a neck injury and was in a lot of pain. We told her we would pray for her healing - and she appreciated it. How cool is that? Mario cared enough about a grumpy stranger to work to make her day better. He treats the people around himself with love and respect and it trickles into every relationship in his life - including mine.

I was lucky enough to learn this lesson while I was single. I was sad that I didn't have someone to show love to at the time. I eventually came to realize I needed to show love to everyone. I needed to smile at the grumpy worker at the post office. Let another car go ahead of me. Send a kind text message to a friend having a rough day. All of those little acts of love make an enormous difference. "For this is the message you have heard from the beginning; we should love one another" (1 John 3:11). The more love we give, the better we feel. We were designed to love!

The Problem with Today's Dating Culture

A marriage cannot thrive without love, and God is love (1 John 4:8). Therefore, a marriage cannot thrive without Christ. You know how it is out there. Our culture neglects incorporating God into the equation. We are afraid to speak His name in our schools. We are afraid to pray publicly. We are afraid to express our beliefs out of fear we will be deemed "bigoted," "judgmental" or "stuck in the past."

There is a problem with aligning our actions with the

way of the world. While it may bring us instant satisfaction, it is not sustainable. It never leads to long-term contentment. It never leads to peace. I like to compare following God's will to a little child crossing the street. The child wants to run across as fast as he or she can. The parent wants to hold hands.

"No!" The child resists, not wanting to be restrained or bound down. But the truth is, the parent isn't trying to prevent the child from crossing the street. The parent is trying to protect the child by guiding him or her at a time when he or she may or may not make it to the other side safely. Recall a time when your parents prevented you from doing something as a child in order to make sure you would be safe. How did you feel in that moment? How do you feel in hindsight?

Rules aren't put in place to limit us. They were created to assist us, free us, and enable us to become the person we each were created to be. Our culture frowns upon rules- especially the ones taught by the Church. Those rules require sacrifice and denial of self: two things that contribute to real love. Sure, you don't always achieve a great amount of momentary pleasure but the everlasting joy you will feel is overwhelming.

When I was a little kid, I knew exactly how dating and relationships worked. Two people meet, they go to dinner and movies for dates and then fall in love. Once they fall in love, they get married. Shortly after, either a stork comes to their house or God magically surprises the couple with a baby. (I wasn't quite sure which!) Everyone is excited, and they all live happily ever after.

The end. The end of that mentality occurred for me around the time I graduated high school. During high school, I slowly learned how babies came to be and that relationships were more complex than they appear in the movies. I still maintained a very innocent view of relationships which was destroyed on June 3rd 2010. Why do I remember the exact date? I have no idea. It was just your average summer day. I was a few days away from officially graduating high school when I was texting a guy friend I was interested in. I was attracted to him because of his heavy involvement in the church. His faith was strong and I learned so much from him about the Catholic faith. Being friends with him dramatically increased my own faith and relationship with Jesus Christ. Before knowing this person, church attendance felt like an option if I had nothing "better" planned rather than something to do every single Sunday. I would never have fathomed voluntarily going to church during a weekday! But this friend's influence taught me the beauty of the Mass along with God's healing power. I had never met any young guy so strong in faith and devoted to the Lord. I thought, "This HAS to be him! This *has* to be the man I am going to marry. There's no way I could find anyone better and more devoted to Christ." I thought wrong. Totally wrong.

In a world where it feels like everyone and everything is so far from being focused on God, it can be easy to become too excited about the people and things that do show him honor. This is why we must always put Christ first, following His will before our own. Even the best people have the potential to lead us astray. God never will.

I was texting this friend about how our days went, life, and other various things when somehow the topic of premarital sex came up. Until that time. I thought premarital sex was for "bad people." Since I was trying to be good and follow Christ's teachings, I assumed the same was true for every other practicing Catholic. This person then shared with me that they had previous sexual relationships. I was crushed. I cannot even express the pain I felt at that moment. I still feel that pain today, years later, when I think about it.

Why would someone else's sexual past have that profound of an impact on me? It hurt for two main reasons. First of all, at the time, I was convinced this person was going to be my husband. How could I marry him now? While I had put a lot of effort into ensuring I would be completely pure for my future spouse, praying for him and our future relationship before we even met, he was sleeping with other people? It hurt. Deeply. After reading the stories of Mary Magdalene and the Prodigal Son about twenty times, I realized that his past was something I had to get over. I learned a lesson on forgiveness, which was very freeing.

The number one reason the information hurt me though: I realized, if this person, as good as he is, as devoted to Christ as he is, could fall into that sin - so could anybody. If someone following Christ's teachings wouldn't be free from that temptation - imagine all of the people who **don't** care about Christ's plan who are having sex prior to marriage. It shocked me. It concerned me. It hurt.

As I've said, the pain never really passed away. But as the years went by I began to understand how destructive it is to fall into sexual sins from a variety of perspectives - (as a family member, as a friend, and as myself.) Premarital sexual relations are a sure-fire way to bring pain and sorrow into relationships. This is why I am passionate about educating others on the reasoning behind Christ's teachings and the joy you will experience by following His will as closely as possible.

Sex Before Marriage:

Why Not?

"Sex before marriage is bad, it *says so* in the Bible." We've all heard it before. Maybe your parents told you? Maybe you heard it at church? Maybe you heard other people say it? Regardless of whether or not you agree or disagree, it is important to learn the reasons behind why the Bible, "says so." As with any Church teaching, I would recommend educating yourself on the reasoning behind why certain actions or behaviors are deemed as sinful or immoral. Everything the Church teaches has intentionality and purpose. If you do not agree with the reasoning behind the teaching, at least be aware of the facts. Blessed Archbishop Fulton Sheen was quoted as saying, "There are not one hundred people in the United States who hate the Catholic Church, but there are millions who hate what they wrongly perceive the Catholic Church to be." That is absolutely true.

One of the biggest topics that I have noticed people neglect to learn enough about is premarital sex. Again, remember the rules are put in place to help us become the best we can be, not to hinder us. There are many physical, relational, and spiritual dangers that come as a result of having premarital sexual relations. Physically, AIDS and other sexually transmitted diseases are always a worry outside of monogamous, married relationships. If an unmarried couple conceives, many lives are affected. Having a child dramatically affects your life, your partner's life and the lives of your family members. There is also a high likelihood the child will have to grow up outside of a two-parent home (this means growing up outside of the family structure God intended). That's if your child is **lucky.** Abortion is a common result of unplanned pregnancies from premarital sexual relationships. Many people give themselves a false sense of security by "using protection" a.k.a. some form of birth control to "stay safe." While "safe sex" may help prevent pregnancies and diseases, it is important to remember the only truly safe sex is abstinence. Abstinence is where a couple never has to have the burden of worrying about unintended consequences for their actions. God loves us and wants to spare us from pain and heartache. He wants to fill us with peace and make us whole; that is precisely why we are suppose to flee from sin. Sin separates. It separates us from Christ, severs relationships with family, and separates us from the people around us. This happens all while leading other people into the same destruction too.

Consider this: if someone is okay with having sex prior to the lifelong commitment of marriage, that means they accept sexual relations outside of the marriage bond. If this person accepts sex outside of marriage before they are married, what would be different once they are married? Acceptance of sex before marriage is a pre-cursor for infidelity in the future. Conversely, when a man and woman persevere through the struggles of maintaining self-control; trust and respect are built. By conducting themselves this way, each person gains more confidence that their boyfriend or girlfriend truly respects them and cherishes their intimacy.

As soon as a person has sex before marriage, all of their future relationships become affected. Entering into a marriage with previous sexual partners automatically affects the intimacy of the married couple. If only one partner has waited until marriage, he or she will have to deal with the feeling that intimacy was not important enough for the other to wait for it. Naturally, comparisons can be made. Whether good or bad, real or perceived, comparisons between spouses and "former lovers" can be extremely detrimental to a relationship. I have a friend who is still dealing with difficulty over her husband's sexual past. They've been married for over 20 years and it still remains a struggle in their relationship.

As with any sin, if a person has failed or has messed up we are forgiven and healed. This works well as long as we move forward and refrain from committing the sin again. Unfortunately, many people have a skewed view of virginity. People think once it is gone, it is gone, there is no turning back. You've "lost" something. Perhaps you have lost some of your innocence and your relationships have changed. The good news is that you've gained an opportunity to grow. A chance to move on. A time to lean on Christ more than ever, to open your heart and allow Him to transform you. It is difficult, but totally possible. I 100% completely advocate saving yourself for marriage. However, I find it even more admirable meeting someone who has messed up in the past, learned from their mistakes, and has moved on, recommitting themselves to a life centered on Christ, and actually following through with it. That is the key. We are human. We sin. We are forgiven with God's mercy. We have grace. We need to use our free will to choose to allow Christ in. "The spirit is willing but the flesh is weak." We cannot do it all on our own. We are weak. We need a savior. The issue typically is found in justification. We justify our actions to make them appear harmless in our minds. I want to take a moment to respond to some of the most common justifications I have heard people use regarding sex outside of the marriage bond.

"But we're in love!"

Sound familiar? If a couple is truly in love in the sense of God's definition of love, they would realize true love requires patience. It does not cater to his or her own desires or pleasures, and does not take delight in evil (1 Corinthians 13). True love would be patient in waiting until marriage. It would demonstrate self-control by not giving into momentary desires, and would not make excuses or justifications in the behavior. We are told there is no greater love than dying for your friends (John 15:13). True love requires dying to oneself for the benefit of the other person. To answer the question - no! Being "in love" is not an acceptable reason to have sex before marriage.

"But we are going to be married one day anyway!"

First of all, you know what happens when you assume: let's just say, nothing good. The couple is not living in reality. Even if the couple is engaged to be married, they are still not married. As I mentioned previously, if a person cannot hold themselves back to maintain morals before he or she is married, why would this person be expected to change once he or she is actually married?

"The Church is outdated. Nobody waits anymore. It's not a big deal."

It's not a big deal when everything is going well. However, sex bonds a man and woman in a very powerful way. When there comes a time when the relationship should end, naturally, the couple will still cling to it as they are so strongly intertwined emotionally. The couple becomes bound into an unhealthy relationship by their sin. After breaking up, the emotional damage can prevent people from being as open and ready for a relationship in the future. Have you ever met someone who was hurt in the past? They usually have difficulty opening up to someone new. Sex plays a huge role in that. To make things more difficult, if a child enters the world through the relationship, the two will have to maintain contact forever. This can be emotionally burdensome on the couple, the child, and all future romantic partners.

"We love each other very much and sex is a way we can express that love."

Very true - in the context of marriage. Prior to that, there are many other ways love can be expressed. Refraining from sexual activity prior to marriage enables the couple to find other ways to express love. Inventiveness is cultivated as couples are challenged to get creative and express themselves in other, non destructive ways. Alice Fryling put it well in an article with the title, "Why Wait for Sex?" when she wrote, "Genital sex is an expression of intimacy, not the means to intimacy. True intimacy springs from verbal and emotional communion. True intimacy is built on a commitment to honesty, love and freedom. True intimacy is not primarily a sexual encounter. Intimacy, in fact, has almost nothing to do with our sex organs. A prostitute may expose her body, but her relationships are hardly intimate." Anyone can become physically intimate, but it takes a special connection to spend the time and energy essential to creating new ways to love each other.

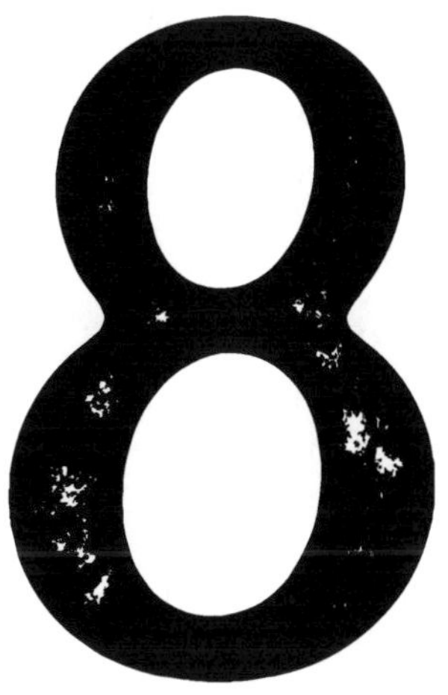

Sex Before Marriage:

Benefits of Waiting

It can be easy to focus on the negative aspects of premarital sex, so let's take a look at some of the positive benefits of waiting:

1. It grows and strengthens the bond of friendship.

Physical intimacy can give the illusion of emotional closeness when the couple is actually not as close as they might think. Without conversations, shared interests, and mutual morals, a relationship will never last. By taking sex out of the equation, nothing about the other person becomes distorted, so the two have the ability to get a clear view of who the other person is and what he or she is passionate about.

2. It allows for good communication during the time of dating.

Without being focused on pleasure and the physical side of a relationship, a couple is able to better focus on the joy of sharing life experiences together. Deeper conversations are able to take place and differences can be discussed and worked through prior to connecting in a physical way.

3. It encourages better, more positive relationships with both sets of parents.

When a couple has to hide their sexual relations from their parents, naturally their level of guilt and stress grows. If the two are waiting, they have nothing to hide or worry about, enabling them to grow in friendship and relatability to their own parents and to the parents of their significant other.

4. The couple can feel free to question whether or not the relationship should continue.

As discussed previously, sexual relationships strongly unite people which can lead to the couple feeling "trapped" in a relationship that they would like to end, but is prolonged due to physical attraction or the need for security. On the other hand, in a relationship where a couple is practicing abstinence, the two are able to see more clearly and break the emotional bond easier if need be. The two are empowered. If they choose to remain in the relationship, they are fully free to do so.

5. Generosity is fostered as opposed to selfishness.

When men and women respect each other, their love matures. They are able to set aside their own desires for the good of the other. Sexual relationships can lead people to feel like they are competing with others their partner may find more attractive. It breeds insecurity and selfishness. Upon becoming sexually intimate, the natural tendency is to continue asking for more and more. If a person is able to set aside their desires before marriage, they have a higher likelihood of doing the same within their marriage.

6. The couple is more likely to have a long-lasting marriage.

Marriage isn't easy - no matter who you are or what your background is. When a couple waits for marriage, they must persevere through struggle and practice self-sacrifice; two important qualities of maintaining a healthy marriage that lasts a lifetime. Self-denial is imperative at times in marriage. Sacrificing free time and leisurely activities to help with a project around the house, or deciding who's family to spend a holiday with are examples of occasions where a decision may need to be made for the benefit of your spouse. There are also times that a married couple will have to abstain from sex during marriage (most commonly) for health related issues that arise. Having practiced abstaining before marriage is great practice on learning to show love to one another in non-sexual ways; a skill that needs to be carried into married life.

7. It is the only 100% full proof guarantee against pregnancy and STDs.

This should be self-explanatory but many people forget: pregnancy and STD's are a result of having sex. If you are concerned about these two things know that abstaining is the only 100%, zero risk, guarantee.

8. There is less risk physical, verbal and emotional abuse.

Sex outside of marriage has a strong connection with violence and other forms of abuse. Think about it. If a person wants to enjoy the sexual side of their partner without officially committing to a lifetime with them, they are concerned with their own wants and desires. Abuse is born of selfishness. Abuse results when a person believes their controlling and manipulative behavior will get them what they want.

9. If you do decide to end the relationship, the pain will not be as harsh.

Sexual intimacy is powerful. It bonds us so strongly to our significant other that if a break up comes, the pain is even more intense and devastating. It ruins the friendship. Without sexual activity, a breakup will still be difficult, but the couple will typically heal faster and be able to maintain some sort of friendly contact in the future without fear of past attraction affecting future relationships. It eliminates feelings of regret and guilt.

10. Waiting until marriage gives you freedom.

It can be disconcerting to be intimate with someone while still having to feel uneasy about whether or not that person will actually commit to you for a lifetime. Sex creates an attachment that when broken can cause a lot of emotional distress. Not having that element allows you the freedom to view the relationship with less emotions attached so if you do see any "red flags" or even minor signs that you should end the relationship, you don't have that attachment keeping you in.

11. It honors your future spouse.

Whether or not you have met the person you are going to marry, they are out there somewhere. How cool would it be to be able to say you cared enough about them to wait and set aside your selfish desires for them- even before knowing them? You are also spared from wondering how you compare sexually to other people they have been with and vice versa. It also demonstrates how special and sacred it is to be together sexually since it wasn't something you did with anyone.

You saved that role specifically for your spouse.

Women tend to equate physical intimacy to love with a commitment. Men have the tendency to equate physical intimacy to immediate gratification without commitment. Because of this, women typically experience depression symptoms and go from unhealthy relationship to unhealthy relationship because they are feeling used, unloved, and begin to think they cannot trust anyone. Time after time, they wonder why history keeps repeating itself and consider all guys to be jerks.

A whole series of books could be written on this topic alone. I challenge you to research these benefits more in depth on your own and to educate yourself in greater detail about the statistics and thought process behind the teaching. Saint John Paul II's, "Theology of the Body" and other books/media related to it would be a great resource to look into.

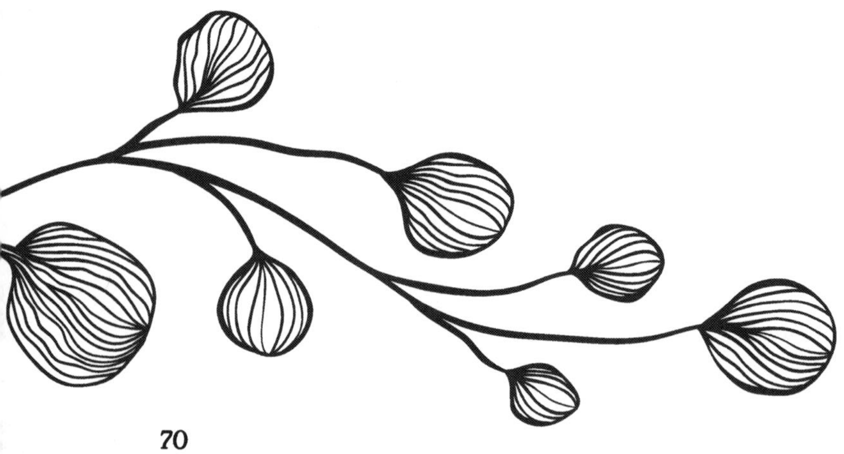

Hookup Culture

Should I use Birth Control?

One of the biggest problems in the dating scene is the normalcy of casual, sexual encounters, also known as the "hook- up culture." Prevalent among students on college campuses, casual sex and instant gratification is encouraged without any type of long-term commitment. It shames, isolates, and disempowers people. It leaves hurt feelings, people feeling sad, regretful, and lost.

The instant gratification, hook-up culture state-of-mind has become the cultural norm in many long-term committed relationships as well. While living together and sleeping together may be the "standard" way of navigating relationships, it is incredibly destructive.

When I was a senior in High School, I went to the doctor for a routine physical check-up. A graduate school student was shadowing my doctor so they both participated in asking me questions.

"Do you smoke?"

"No."

"Do you drink?"

"No."

"Are you sexually active?"

"No."

"In the last 12 months, have you been sexually active?"

"No."

"You know, it is important to be honest about your answers. These questions are asked so we can help you."

“I know.”

Both the doctor and her assistant appeared visibly surprised at my answers and skeptical of my truthfulness. The appointment continued.

“Alright, you are almost good to go! Everything looks great except I see you still need to get your HPV vaccination.”

“Oh, I thought that vaccine was for preventing STD’s.”

“It is. We like to have all of our teenage girls get it, especially before heading off to college, so you should definitely be getting it soon.”

“No, thank you. I’m not going to be sexually active in college so I don’t think I’ll need that.”

Again, more shock. The nurse and nurse assistant proceeded to tell me that while some girls think they are going to wait until marriage to have sex, it never happens. It was a wise decision to be vaccinated so I wont have to worry about the risk of HPV. A mini debate ensued when I persisted in my decision not to take the vaccine, and the appointment ended with the doctors talking to my mom asking her to convince me of the importance of getting vaccinated.

This is very representative of our culture. Instead of encouraging one another to uphold our moral beliefs, we jump to conclusions. "That's impossible! Nobody does that! What an outdated thing to do! Get with the times!" It can be extremely difficult to stay true to our values, even when we know they are right and the best way to live.

Think about how common contraceptive use has become. It is rare for people to even question the morality or potential consequences, since using contraception is the norm. Some wonder if they are so commonly used, why does the Church believe artificial contraceptives are such a problem? The problem with artificial birth control methods (pills, condoms etc.) is that they prevent couples from totally giving themselves to one another without holding back anything, including their fertility. It actually breaks the marriage vows. Contraception says, "I promise to love you for better or for worse, but not for the imagined worse of an additional child." These methods demonstrate a lack of trust that God will provide and also put the control of birth into human hands instead of God's. Of course, we've all seen beautiful families come about regardless of how many children a couple has. But, that still doesn't make it morally acceptable.

A problem with the birth control pill is that it alters the woman's body. It is a medicine for someone who is not sick. Being able to conceive during a woman's child bearing years is a healthy thing. It means the body is functioning normally.

There may be various reasons why a couple may want to postpone or prevent child birth. Perhaps they think they have a lack of adequate finances, or they may already have a hard time managing the children they do have. Whatever it may be, there is always a solution for it. The current Catholic Church teaching is that Natural Family Planning (NFP) is a morally permissible way to space the births of children. This is because Jesus teaches us that love is sacrifice even to the extent of death. When a couple practices NFP, they must die to themselves and their desires periodically when they need to abstain. It is the only form of pregnancy prevention that requires sacrifice. It also requires self-control. It offers the unique opportunity of learning about the way our bodies work and being in tune with one another, deepening the relationship. It still leaves the possibility open for life if God still chooses.

Although NFP is considered to be acceptable according to Church teaching, I personally argue that even NFP can be abused. In the first edition of this book, I only knew about NFP what I had been told. From my understanding, it was a "natural" form of birth control. Now, having experienced married life, neither my husband nor I have taken any action to avoid having children. We have been blessed to have two little ones but we also had two miscarriages. After suffering those losses and getting to know other women (and men) who desparately desire children but cannot conceive, it is clear to me that the ability to bear life is a gift. Each child is a gift- not owed to us simply because we desire one. We can try to make our plans but we will never have total control over our circumstances and precisely when we will have children, how far apart in age they will be etc. It truly comes down to being open to what God is doing in your life. Being able to conceive during your child bearing years is healthy- not an inconvenience to be corrected.

That is my perspective now as a married wife and mother, but many women are encouraged to use birth control before marriage. This can still be harmful because it leads unmarried couples to have a false sense of safety when it comes to preventing pregnancy. It gives the illusion there are no risks involved with sexual activity.

"What about for illnesses?" You may ask. That is a different story. If a pill is needed, not for the purpose of preventing children, it is considered to fit in with Church teaching.

Ultimately, it is important to do your own research and thorough evaluation of your beliefs. When it comes to the decision of using artificial contraceptives, you may benefit from asking yourself:

1. *Is this increasing my relationship with God? Will this help lead my partner to heaven?*
2. *Am I making this decision out of convenience or fear? Or out of love and truth?*

3. Have I researched why the Church maintains it's stance on the matter?

4. Will this glorify my body and help me become the best version of my self, enabling me to live up to my fullest potential?

I encourage you to put this to prayer. Each woman's circumstances are varying and unique, but from my personal experience, never using contraceptives or family planning methods in my marriage has been unifying and freeing.

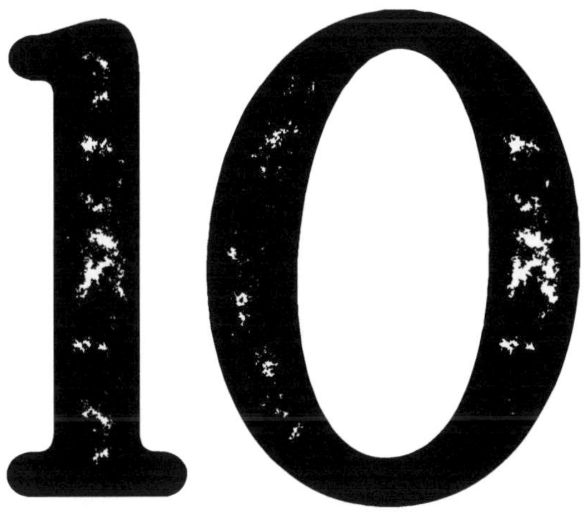

Cohabitation

The majority of people don't claim to be a "bad" person nor do they truly desire to do the wrong thing. What I've noticed has been happening in our culture looks like this: people have the illusion they are doing the "right" thing even though it is totally wrong. Certain immoral behaviors have been normalized in our society to the point that most people think what they are doing is harmless. The basic "system" of dating, for example, has become so common, people don't even realize what they are doing wrong. Dating relationships today commonly look like this:

1. You feel empty, like something is missing.

2. You decide this missing piece is a significant other. You look for one in all of the normal places; school, work, parties, bars and online.

3. Once you meet someone with mutual interests and mutual attraction is there, you continue hanging out with them until you're sure you want some kind of commitment with them.

4. Once you commit, you continue doing what you're doing: going on dates and having fun together.

5. If your relationship is still going strong at this point, after a while, it feels like you've hit the natural next step; living together. You think it will be a great way to ensure compatibility when you get married, and you will be able to save money on rent. You already spend so much time together anyway, "Why waste gas driving back and fourth?"

In many circumstances, cohabitation leads to a painful breakup. In the circumstances where the couple does end up getting married, a whole new set of struggles arise. It leads to emptiness within your marriage and robs you of the amazing joy to be experienced on your wedding day.

Most people can understand the issues that come as a result of premarital sex, but cohabitation seems to be much trickier to comprehend. When you are living with someone, you are almost always in close proximity with that person. Naturally, you will both begin to grow even closer and more intimate. Because of this, you will likely end up letting your guard down and having sex.

Let's say you aren't having sex. You and your significant other are sleeping in separate rooms and remaining pure. First of all, I would recommend questioning how attracted you are to your significant other if you can remain in such close proximity everyday and have the restraint to stay away from them, even at vulnerable hours of the night. Sharing a home with someone you are highly attracted to and in love with places you in a situation where you are highly vulnerable to temptation. Although there may appear to be some good aspects of trying to remain pure while cohabitating, the problem is that whether it is intentional or unintentional, you are leading other people astray. If a couple is living together, it is commonly assumed they are having sex. Though we cannot live our lives according to how other people may view us or think of us, we are making a statement, through our actions, when we fail to avoid having the appearance of sin. Ephesians 5:3, 1 Thessalonians 5:22, and 1 John 3:18 emphasize this point.

Two of my close friends from college moved in together. From that time on all of our mutual friends (and even a few of their friends that knew I was close to them) repeatedly asked me if they had sex yet. Aside from it being weird that they thought I would know this information, they were curious. When I said the couple claimed they weren't doing anything sexually, everyone said they didn't believe them. When you cohabitate prior to marriage, you are sending a message that you approve of that behavior. You are saying it's okay to "play house."

Living together before you're married is "performance based." Most people want to "try it out" to see if they're compatible. Premarital sex is often compared to test-driving a car before buying it. One major flaw with this argument is that cars are objects meant to be used not loved. If you base your relationship on performance (what they can do for you) as opposed to real love for the individual, then it's set up to fail. "The problem with pre-marital sex and cohabitation isn't that you're going too far, it's that you aren't going far enough," (Jason Evert).

I can't tell you how many friends I know who are waiting and wishing for their live-in boyfriends to propose to them. Typically, it doesn't happen until several years down the road and that is ***if*** it even ends up happening.

When you live with someone before marriage, you are using them. Nobody wants to admit that, but it is the truth. By living together without committing to marriage, you are saying, "I love you, but not enough to spend my whole life with you," and, "I love you, but if I find out you have weird habits and quirks, or snore in your sleep, I want a way out." That's not love. Love is unconditional. Love is saying, "Nothing you ever do will make me stop loving you." That is how I know I am in love with Mario. I am fully aware he is imperfect. I know there will be times he will hurt me. I also know that I am imperfect and there will be instances where I will hurt him. But I am willing - I am willing to do anything it takes to improve his life and guide him closer to God. I have chosen him as the person to spend my life with, have a family with, and remain with forever despite all of the unfavorable conditions life may throw at us.

Many people suggest cohabitation is necessary as a way to save money. Is it too expensive to rent your own place? I have a solution for you. Find a roommate! Actually, find a group of three or four roommates so you can save even more. Do you spend so much time together that it's like you're "practically living together anyway"? Good, you need that time to get to know each other to the point where you can fully commit. Are you "planning on getting married one day anyway?" Nice! While you wait for that to happen you will have something to look forward to. Are you terrified of divorce and want to make sure you've fully tested the relationship, hoping your future marriage won't end up the way your parents' marriage did? Research the statistics on cohabitation.

One of the most exciting aspects of wedding planning was knowing I would finally get to live with Mario. Driving back and forth was not easy, convenient, or fun. But the excitement we had as we would daydream about our new life, our future and living in our new house together, was overwhelming. I knew in advance our wedding night was going to be amazing. It was exciting to be able to lay next to each other knowing that we were finally able to wake up next to one another and live together, not just temporarily, but forever! Most importantly, we have been more appreciative of each other and for those moments because we know what it was like to live without them and to withhold our momentary desires for a greater purpose. I knew Mario loved me, not because of how he physically expressed it to me, but because his authentic love for me and his love for God outweighed his love of catering to his own self. He died to his own wants and desires for my benefit.

That is love.

Potential Person

What are you looking for in a potential significant other? What is important to you? Do you want someone who can make you laugh? Someone tall? Short? Light hair? Dark hair? Interested in the same type of music? Family oriented? What qualities are you looking for?

From an early age, I always wanted to marry someone who was Catholic. They didn't have to be practicing, I just wanted someone who had the same basic belief system as I did. As I grew in faith and had a major turning point in my relationship with Christ, the desire for a Catholic boyfriend became a non-negotiable quality. Chances are, if you are reading this book, you are a person of faith seeking another person of faith. The following are some little bits of wisdom that may help you along the way. Consider how they may be similar to your circumstances and relationships. Learn from my mistakes!

1. Regardless of your faith, relationships work best when both parties have a mutual moral compass.

When it comes to the Christian dating scene, 2 Corinthians 6:14 is typically referenced. "Be not unequally yoked together with unbelievers: for what fellowship hath righteousness with unrighteousness? What communion hath light with darkness?" As I said before, scripture makes statements with specific purpose. When two people have the same (or similar) view of what is right and what is wrong, disputes are less common. When they do occur, it is easier for both parties to determine who was right in a situation and who needs to ask for forgiveness. Having the same viewpoint spares couples from arguing over core values and beliefs. Keep in mind: it is imperative not to enter into a relationship with someone based on having mutual religious beliefs alone. Many factors should contribute to the decision to begin exclusively dating someone.

2. Fall in love with someone for who they are in the present moment. Don't anticipate change!

Do not, I repeat, do **not** fall for a fixer upper! God is the builder - not you! When we are attracted to another person it is easy to begin having wishful thinking. We can slowly form our perception of them in our minds to be how we wish for them to be. This may not be how they actually are or will ever be. We can easily justify unhealthy behaviors and gloss over qualities we find important that the other person lacks.

At one point, I was talking to a guy I thought was my ideal match. My parents thought so too and for a few weeks, my mom went around telling everyone she thought she found my future husband. (She was the one who introduced us.) When this man finally asked me out, my entire family was elated. Seriously, my aunts, cousins, and grandmother spent hours discussing how excited they were at a family party. I was excited, too. This guy was great! He had an awesome personality, was friendly, respectful to elders, family-oriented, into his faith, and he didn't live too far away from me. He was the total package! Once I got to know him better, I learned he smoked cigarettes and used swear words in nearly every one of his sentences. Not to mention, I heard from other friends he was big into partying. As someone who never "partied," coughs like a maniac when around smoke, and cannot stand swear words, it was interesting how magically it didn't seem so bad when ***he*** did it.

I thought, "Well, he has never smoked around me nor has he ever encouraged me to smoke." "If we started dating he would most likely stop getting drunk on Saturday nights." "Sure, he swears, but he never used those words in a bad way. He was just passionate about the subject matter in our conversations." During the moments I would question the character of this potential partner, my family justified him too. "He is so family oriented and driven! His personality is rare these days. Sure, he has a few flaws but you will be such a positive influence on him. He will change! You would be perfect together!"

I wasn't completely sure it was a good idea to get involved with this person but I figured I would hang out with him a few times and give it a shot. Long story short, the friendship was great initially, but quickly faded away. When he cancelled plans and failed to reschedule, I decided to stop pursuing that relationship. Man, am I glad I did! Shortly after, I started seriously talking to my (now) husband, Mario. It was so much easier knowing what Mario was like in the present moment. I didn't have to justify any of his behaviors or try to convince him to change in any way. I loved him for who he was in reality, not who I wanted him to be.

3. Be with someone you aspire to become more like.

Who you spend your time with is who you become. "You are the average of the five people you spend the most time with." – Jim Rohn. You need to surround yourself with people who are doing things better than you are, people who you aspire to be like. Have you ever met someone who has changed significantly after meeting their boyfriend or girlfriend? Have you noticed a change in yourself when hanging around people in different social circles? We are like chameleons. We adapt to our surroundings. This can work in our favor or hurt us. Strive to find someone whose habits are good. They will inevitably rub off on you. Whether or not the relationship becomes long lasting, you will have become a better person as a result of the habits and personality traits the other person has influenced you to possess.

One thing I noticed early on in my relationship with Mario, was that for the first time, I felt like I was with a "better" person than I was. Perhaps "better" isn't the right word. He was stronger in his spiritual life and devotion to Christ. This was something I specifically prayed for in a future spouse. Mario was the first guy I met that I wanted to become like as much as possible. I love the positive way he views life. I admire the way he treats, values, and respects people. I appreciate the way he aspires to grow and improve daily by reading motivational books and Scripture. I commend him for how he doesn't constantly consume unproductive media content, doesn't excessively drink alcohol, and that he is a problem solver. Mutual interests and hobbies come and go, but the way a person views the world and lives their life is long lasting. Many people are fun to go to dinner, bowling, or watch a movie with. The person you want to be committed to forever must excite you on another level. This person must make you evaluate your own life in order to strive to become the best you can be - the best version of yourself!

4. Look for any red flags.

Keyword: any! Red flags go unnoticed in relationships all the time. Why? We block them out. We don't want them to be true. We figure, everyone has flaws so there are some qualities we can overlook. Being aware of red flags is crucial to our overall well-being. Do not let them go unnoticed! We have instincts for a reason. Trust your gut! If something feels uncomfortable or wrong, it probably is. A few of the most common examples of red flags are:

Verbal Abuse

Does the person you are with make you feel bad about yourself in any way? They are critical about your appearance, personality, interests, or people who you hold close. They don't support you in your successes nor when things are tough. It wasn't until after I ended a relationship type friendship with someone that I realized how verbally abusive he had been. For instance, I remember one day my skin was broken out a little bit. Makeup helped. But you could still tell my skin wasn't 100% flawless. I almost called the guy to say I couldn't come hang out with him that day, however I looked in the mirror and told myself I was overreacting. "This person claims he loves me and thinks the world of me. He probably doesn't even notice these minor imperfections the way I do." So I went to meet him. I remember we took a walk at a park and we were sitting facing each other at a picnic table. The afternoon was going really well. But then he said, "Did you ever think about trying out that new grapefruit facial wash they are always showing on TV commercials?"

Surely, he wasn't referencing my skin. "Yeah! I actually have that one, it smells so good, I love it!" I replied.

"Really? That's weird. Well you should start using it again."

"I used it last night."

"Then why does your skin look so bad?"

My heart sunk. Not only did he notice but he pointed it out. I tried my hardest to hold back tears.

I brushed the incident off thinking he was trying to help me. I thought, "He just wants me to become the best person I can be. That's why he doesn't want me to have any minor flaws even if they are temporary!" Terrible logic! Perhaps one of these instances can be brushed off, but it continued to happen.

"You would be really attractive if you were taller, and you had a tan."

"You're always so conservative. I don't understand why you don't drink. You need to loosen up and let your guard down. You would be more fun." (I was under 21 at the time).

"I wish you would show off your body more. If you toned up a little bit and wore more revealing clothes, you would look good."

There were many other times this person made condescending remarks about me, my appearance, my clothes, my hobbies, my friends, and my family. I totally brushed it off at the time. Listen: don't let things go. Don't settle for someone who treats you like garbage. Wait for the guy, the man, who would never dream of insulting you.

Physical Abuse

Physical abuse occurs when a person is hurting you in any kind of physical way. Firm grabbing, hitting, punching, destroying your belongings, forcing you to have sex, threatening to harm you in any way, even in a joking manner, all of those are signs of physical abuse. If you ever begin to see signs of these behaviors, run away! The earlier the better in these circumstances. It may be hard, but you cannot be afraid of breaking off a relationship that is harmful or life-threatening to you. Abusive behavior is inexcusable. You will find someone who will treat you with love and respect. Don't be afraid to lose or leave someone who isn't elevating your self esteem and making you feel confident and loved as the person you are.

Manipulative Behavior

It is important to be aware of any manipulative behavior in general. I was once talking to a guy who would get mad whenever I spent time with my friends. He was always out with his friends. But when I would spend time with mine he became angry. He couldn't trust me even when I assured him I was simply shopping or eating out with friends. If I wasn't able to answer his nightly phone call, then he would become mad and tell me how hurt he was. Conversely, there were several times ***he*** was unable to talk but he never thought that was a big deal.

There's a line in the song, "Somebody That I Use to Know" by Gotye, that says, "Now and then I think of all the times you [treated me disrespectfully] but had me believing it was always something that I'd done." That is how manipulation works. The **other** person hurts **you** and somehow **you** are the one who ends up apologizing. They constantly twist things around so you feel you aren't measuring up. You begin to feel bad. In order to make amends, you cave in and allow them to have their way. The deadly cycle keeps going.

5. Close family members and friends don't like your partner.

Your family and friends love you and want the best for you. If they don't think you should be with a boyfriend, they are probably right. Be open to their opinions. If they are telling you the person you are with is a jerk or that you deserve better, LISTEN TO THEM! When we're in love, a shiny ray of goodness shines upon our beloved. It is a good thing when it comes to your spouse, but when you are in an unhealthy relationship, it can be a recipe for disaster.

6. Make sure nothing is hidden or complicated.

If a relationship has to be hidden, it is not a healthy relationship. If you are in a relationship where you are "dating but not officially dating," cut it off immediately. Seriously. I've experienced friend after friend in tears over a relationship that was "official but unofficial." I've been in a relationship like that myself. Trust me: no matter how hard you justify, or want to convince yourself it is a good idea, it is never a good idea. A secret relationship prevents you from fully being free (Luke 8:17). All it will cause is pain and confusion.

Why would someone be in love and not want to share that joy and excitement with the people around them? Privacy is different than secrecy. If a person likes to keep relationships private, that means they don't want other people budding into their personal business. If they want the relationship to be secret it means they are hiding something. They can promise you they aren't hiding anything all they want to. But they are. It is just the truth. As Dr. Phil once said, "People who have nothing to hide, hide nothing." Run away from the relationship. Your significant other must be okay with the relationship being completely transparent.

I was recently talking to a friend about her new significant other. After sharing how they met, she told me they were "taking things slow" and seeing how it goes. They are basically boyfriend and girlfriend, but not officially. Wow. While that mentality is becoming normal these days, it is scary to me. When you meet someone you are in love with, someone you are crazy about, someone whose needs you place above your own, it brings so much joy and excitement! So much, that you never want to hide it or restrain it in any way.

Relationships should be simple. Beware of hidden or complicated relationships.

7. Do not enter an exclusive relationship unless you are truly interested in potentially marrying this person.

This is one thing I've always had a difficult time understanding. Why would someone want to be in a relationship with someone they do not see themselves with in their future? What is the point of exclusivity in that case? Pride and selfishness. If the plan is ultimately marriage, the couple is practicing for the exclusive relationship they will have within their marriage. Without marriage as a future intention, the couple is exclusive merely because they want the other person all to their self. It is a very possessive type of relationship. True love is not self seeking. Once you enter an exclusive relationship, it is hard to get out. After being boyfriend and girlfriend, spending lots of time together in a more connected way, it is emotionally difficult to get out if you realize the person you are with isn't someone you would like to be with forever in a marriage commitment.

December 17th, 2014 is another notable day to me.

I spent nearly all of my life with the desire to find a significant other. Finally, I met a guy who seemed perfect! He had every one of the qualities I deemed non-negotiable in a future spouse. Beyond that, he was a fantastic person. Kind, funny, heavily involved in Church activities, just an all around awesome guy. For once interest was mutual and it was super exciting for me. Our mutual friends thought we would be great together.

However, as respectful as this person treated me and as much as I liked him, I couldn't shake the feeling that I was uncertain about marrying him. I can't fully explain why - just a subtle feeling in the pit of my stomach. This was troubling to me. Finally, I meet this amazing guy, everything is great except I can't imagine myself marrying him. I took the situation to prayer. Every time I prayed it seemed he was not the one for me. I wanted to resist that. I thought, "I've waited long enough to find someone and now I've met someone great. We are both interested in each other. But now, I like everything about him *except* the idea of marrying him? Am I just nervous? Should I wait to think about marriage or a long-term commitment once we've been dating for a while?" I was confused and frustrated. I decided to continue getting to know this person better and being his friend. Maybe over time my feelings of uneasiness would change.

One night before we went out to dinner, he told me how he felt. He asked me if I wanted to "make things official" between us. I couldn't believe it! I was elated and honored to have such a wonderful person interested in me. I couldn't wait to experience what a healthy relationship would be like. You have no idea how much I had hoped, wished, and prayed for that moment to come! I thought about my answer for a second and realized to say yes would be using this person. Sure, I wasn't looking for any physical intimacy or sexual gratification. But I was appealing to my desires of having a wonderful, Catholic guy as a boyfriend and being in an exclusive relationship. I cared about this person enough that I didn't want to mess around with his emotions. I didn't want to waste his time just so I could have my first official boyfriend. I told him the truth, as difficult as it was to do. I was unable to agree to a mutually exclusive relationship, but I was interested in him and open to the possibility in the future.

I needed more time to get to know him better and to see how our relationship would evolve. It was difficult at the time, especially when I wanted to be in a relationship more than anything. But let me tell you - it was a wonderful decision! It truly pays to be honest about your feelings with anyone you will potentially date. Were his feelings hurt in the moment? Probably. But it is beautiful for me to see him now, happily married and knowing I never interfered with him meeting his wife. Doing the moral and right thing frees us.

8. Make sure you are prayerfully compatible.

One of the few reasons I didn't feel fully confident in beginning an exclusive relationship with the person in the previous story, was because I didn't feel comfortable praying with him. He was the first guy who *actually* wanted to incorporate prayer into our relationship which was huge to me. However, the prayers always felt forced from my end. I always wanted him to do the praying because somehow I was always at a loss for what to say. I had trouble opening up.

As I prepared for marriage with Mario, we were both surprised to learn it is common for couples to feel uncomfortable praying together. We are very fortunate to have established a mutual "prayer life" if you will, very early on in our relationship. Our spirituality is the same and our prayer style is very similar so praying comes naturally to us. We've integrated it into our lives to become a daily habit-sometimes even multiple times a day. It has been instrumental in growing and strengthening our bond.

Prayer gets us through the difficult times and helps us rejoice in the exciting moments. A friend once posed the question, "What is the most intimate thing a man can do with a woman?" The answer was prayer. That couldn't be truer. But isn't it interesting? It is often easier for people to strip down and get naked than it is to strip down emotionally and share the intimate thoughts residing at the very core of who we are.

9. Don't settle out of loneliness or desperation.

Never, ever settle out of loneliness. Never settle out of

fear you will never find anyone else or anyone better. Relationships don't work because someone has found the perfect person. They work when both parties are committed and willing to love as Christ loves - selflessly. I believe the Lord ultimately guides each of us to the person we need to be with. But we cannot expect everything to magically fall into place when we find "the one." We need to build our own character. We need to prepare and equip ourselves to best love and serve our beloved. At the same time, it is important that your significant other have their own standards. Be sure they aren't merely appeasing yours.

10. Ask: Will this person get me to heaven?

As a Christian, ultimately our goal is to get to heaven. In marriage, our goal is to get our spouse to heaven. Will your potential spouse get you to heaven? Do they want you to grow in holiness and love of neighbor? Do they encourage you to go to Mass with them? Do they think Mass interferes with their weekend plans? Are they accepting of your beliefs? Or are they critical? Do they respect and value you? Be with someone who wants you to be closer to God. Be with someone who is on a mission to get you to heaven.

Dating with Purpose

Preparing for marriage doesn't begin when you're engaged or even in the dating phase. It begins long before entering into a relationship. When we are single and feeling lonely it is easy to grow frustrated while waiting for someone to pop into your life. The thing is, you aren't waiting. You're preparing. Remember that. If you constantly tell yourself you are lonely and miserable in your singleness, then you will actually feel lonely and miserable. If you realize you are a happy, whole individual working on becoming the best person you can possibly be (which means you're prepared for a relationship), then you will be happy and full of joy. When you feel joyful and content, you will exude that positivity. You want to date a happy person, right? Well, so does your potential significant other! Become someone that your future significant other will gravitate toward.

The best way to attract a good person is to become one! As many people will say, "you can't look for love-love finds you when you're not looking." That's often how it happens. The simple truth is that you will be introduced and open to that special person when you are ready, when you truly become the best version of yourself. While for several years of my young adult life I thought I was perfectly ready, I really wasn't. We need to be completely comfortable with who we are as individuals and as strong as we can be in our relationship with Christ.

Dating Around

The term "dating around" comes with a negative connotation. We typically visualize it as leading several people on, being physically intimate, possibly entering into an exclusive relationship, and ultimately ending awkwardly. This can leave both parties feeling hurt, lost, and left with many mixed emotions. It doesn't have to be that way! All romantic relationships end in a breakup until you meet the one you commit to for a lifetime. I've learned is that it is possible to end a friendship with a person of the opposite sex on good terms. The secret: staying pure in your actions together.

I am very lucky that I realized the destructiveness of physical activity prior to marriage. Once you've become passionate with someone your relationship changes forever. I'm not just talking about sex. This includes anything more than a friendly peck. Anything more than that and it is almost always awkward between the two of you if the relationship ends. It is so freeing for me to know I can still be cordial with former interested guy friends. Specifically, the ones where there was some type of romantic interest involved. I don't have to worry about having lingering feelings, attachments, or any kind of physical past.

Free yourself! Get to know more men for who they are as people. They are individuals with dignity and value. Learn how the minds of men tend to be. Nourish friendships with the women in your life or Church community. It is important to have friends who share your values and know your goals and desires so they can help give you guidance and input along the way.

It's like Learning to Ride a Bike

Do you remember when you first learned to ride a bike? After bravely rejecting the training wheels, it's time for your mom or dad to give you that big push. Before you know it, you're on your own. You're finally doing it! The wind is blowing. You're moving fast. There is a big smile on your face. You feel the rush! You are riding your bike for the first time!

Caught up in the excitement, you suddenly realize you are forgetting an important detail - how to stop. Uh oh! Panic sets in. Next thing you know, you're on the ground sobbing. As your parent wipes away the tears, attempting to comfort you. You have two decisions. You have the option to either; give up bike riding forever or get back up and start over again.

In John 8:3-11, we hear the story of a group of teachers of the law and Pharisees who bring an adulterous woman in front of Jesus. They tell Him what the woman did and asked Him what His opinion was in the situation. The scribes and Pharisees intentionally did this as a way to test Jesus in an attempt to use His words and teachings against Him. Keep in mind, according to their law, her sins were grounds for being stoned.

"He who is without sin among you, let him be the first to throw a stone at her."

Great answer, Jesus. He then rhetorically asks the woman if any of the scribes and Pharisees have condemned her after hearing His belief on stoning the woman for her sins. When the woman tells Jesus no one has condemned her, He says, "Then neither do I condemn you." He instructs the woman to, "Go and sin no more."

Much like learning to ride a bike, we must get up after falling, wipe away the tears, get back on track, and keep moving forward. If we continue to live in our sinfulness just because we already messed up, we would be an adult riding a bike with training wheels. Not only would that be embarrassing, but it would be hard to get to our destinations quickly.

Allowing our sinfulness to define us and direct our behavior is a straight up lie from the devil. It is. We often forget, God is on our team. He's that parent rooting for us. He's the one who runs to our side when we hit a large stick and fly off of our bike. He's the one who instructs us to wear a helmet - despite the fact that it's "uncool," "uncomfortable" or we "just don't want to."

The Lord gives us safety measures for our soul, paralleling the rules our parents put in place when we are learning to ride our bike for the same exact reason: love for us. Stop trying to resist that love.

Maybe you had a painful breakup? You trusted a person who left you feeling hurt, used, and damaged. You got caught up in an exciting moment at a party and acted in a way you now regret. Maybe you went a little too far physically with your boyfriend. Perhaps you watched a movie you know you shouldn't have, or breached the trust of someone you cared about. Maybe your marriage didn't work out the way you anticipated it to.

Regardless of the mistakes we've made, or things we wish would have happened differently - we truly have the chance to start anew. The whole point of our faith is that Jesus died so that we could live eternally, without being bound and imprisoned by our sins. He already freed us. The hard work is done. It is up to us to get back up on our bikes no matter how many times we fall off and keep going.

But how?

In terms of relationships, I have found that the three pillars of Lent; almsgiving, fasting, and prayer have doubled for me as what I also like to call: the three pillars of self-control. There are three different areas that, when strengthened, helped tremendously in maintaining self-control. Another way to phrase the three pillars of self-control are sacrificing, giving, and prayer.

1. Sacrificing

When we think of "sacrifice" the first thing that often comes to mind is Jesus on the Cross. In regard to self-control, I like to think of sacrifice as intentionally refraining from participating in something I enjoy. Why do I choose to deny myself in this way, you ask? Well, I've learned that it frees me. Just like Jesus' suffering freed us.

When I was dating Mario, occasionally kissing would become too prolonged. We weren't doing anything *terribly* wrong but we were going too far for our standards. Mario suggested we stop kissing altogether for a while. I agreed it was a good idea, as quick pecks can easily lead to a lengthy make-out session, but simultaneously, I was annoyed.

"This stinks." I thought. "Why can't he just want us to limit it to quick kisses instead of refraining 100%?" I knew Mario's suggestion was the right thing to do, but I didn't like it. It was hard.

So, we did it. Eventually we started being able to kiss again and this time, it was a lot easier to keep it quick.

Periodically, we went back to taking breaks from kissing again and although it was never fun, it allowed us to never come close to removing our clothes or going way too far.

Mario could have easily said, "Well, we've already kissed a lot, so it doesn't make sense to hold it back." But he was determined to ensure we would be able to uphold the values we preached and believed in.

The same is true in any circumstance. Do not allow your past failings to define the person you are in the present moment. Fast from the actions, habits, and people that are leading you to fall. Get back on that bike, and continue moving forward! "Go and sin no more."

2. Giving

I tend to enjoy sticking to myself. I "recharge" from having some alone time. There is a healthy balance, though, between needing some alone time and excluding oneself from community. Noticeably, this behavior is common of both singles and couples. Singles tend to isolate themselves after a breakup. They hang around people who are familiar and comfortable out of fear of rejection or loneliness. Couples often cling to each other and isolate themselves when they initially enter into a relationship.

Mario and I met while volunteering at our church. During our dating days, we remained involved in our church community. Beyond that, we did service projects together, and established a group of mutual friends. As we gave to our church and our community, we received a ton of support, encouragement, and accountability.

When I was single, I eventually learned I needed to get involved with groups, meet new people, and give of myself to the world around me. Gifting others with support, assistance, and love adds value to their lives and helps keep you on track. How can you give of your time, talents and treasures as an individual? How can you give as a couple?

3. Prayer

The third pillar of self-control is prayer. Pray for the grace to be strong in moments of temptation. Ask for courage, restraint, peace; anything you need to get back on the good and righteous path. He will give it to you!

The Importance of Prayer

It is essential to establish some sort of prayer routine. Your prayer style and structure will most likely evolve over time. That's a good thing! It signifies you are growing in your relationship with Christ. If you are new to the Church or not use to incorporating prayer into your daily life this could feel intimidating. But fear not! It is simple! Spend some time praying in a variety of different ways. This is the best way to determine which style(s) you are most comfortable with. This will also help you on your faith journey in your life. The following are some suggestions for improving your prayer life.

» Making a habit of praying first thing when you wake up

» Making a habit of reflecting upon the day and praying right before going to sleep

» Praying throughout the day, in both the peaceful moments and stressful ones

» Joining a prayer group

» Reading Scripture (even if it is only a verse or paragraph a day.)

» Praying the Rosary

» Reading spiritual books

» Listening to religious audio books or Podcasts

» Singing or listening to Christian music

» Creating or viewing religious art

» Bible journaling

» Watching faith based movies

» Volunteering to help a group or a person in need

» Attending weekday Mass

The possibilities are endless. There is a Latin phrase, "Orare est laborare, laborare est orare; "to work is to pray." Everything we do is a form of prayer. Our very lives are a form of prayer!

Prepare Yourself

Have you ever heard the saying, "You find love when you stop looking" or "You don't look for love, love comes to you?" There is a great deal of truth in those statements! Until you realize God is the provider of all of the love you need, you will constantly be searching for something or someone you will never find.

Strive for growth and improvement. Attack your fears and face your insecurities head on. Expand your capacity to love and to be loved. Elevate the people around you by assisting them in their needs, complimenting and encouraging them. Look for ways you can make the lives of others better. Cultivate a spirit of gratitude and appreciation for all you have been given. Seek out your enemies and learn to love them.

Embrace your time of singleness. Be intentional in your relationships. Embrace every moment as an opportunity to glorify God by rejoicing in successes and persevering during the struggles. Become content in your own self. Contentment comes from within. True joy comes from Jesus Christ. You have already been given all of the resources you need. Actively and intentionally prepare yourself to love as Jesus loved. What are you waiting for? Make use of each and every beautiful moment of life. **Prepare!**

Kenzie & Mario's Wedding Day

About the Author

A graduate of La Roche University and passionate about her Catholic faith, Kenzie has great enthusiasm for encouraging others to live more fulfilling lives of goodness and virtue. She married her husband, Mario, in May of 2016. She shares her thoughts about faith and motherhood through her online social media platform, **The Overnight Mom.**

Let's Connect:

theovernightmom.com

If you enjoyed this book, it would be appreciated if you leave a review on Amazon– Thank you!

Bibliography

Teresa, and Lucinda Vardey. A Simple Path. New York: Ballantine, 1995. Print.

Bartels, F. K. "The Catholic Church: Gift of Love, Truth and Life - Living Faith - Home & Family - News - Catholic Online." The Catholic Church: Gift of Love, Truth and Life - Living Faith - Home & Family - News - Catholic Online. Http://www.catholic.org/, 23 Jan. 2011. Web. 21 June 2016.

Kimbra. Somebody That I Use to Know. Gotye. Wally De Backer, 2011. MP3.

Scripture Passages are taken from: The New American Bible, Revised Edition (NABRE): http://www.usccb.org/bible/

Badwal, Penny. "When Too Far Is Not Far Enough." Http://www.cam.org.au/. Catholic Archdiocese of Melbourne, 24 June 2011. Web. 21 June 2016.

Groth, Aimee. "You're The Average Of The Five People You Spend The Most Time With." Business Insider. Business Insider, Inc, 24 July 2012. Web. 21 June 2016.

Fryling, Alice. "Why Wait for Sex?A Look at the Lies We Face." Why Wait for Sex? Student Leadership Journal, 1995. Web. 13 July 2016.

Notes

Notes

Thank You

...from the bottom of my heart for reading this book. My hope is that it opened your mind and heart to a change in perspective. Always remember that it is only when we make all of our decisions out of love, rather than fear, that we will find peace.

I will be praying for you.

Made in the USA
Columbia, SC
11 February 2021